A KID'S GUIDE TO GROWING...

HERBS

Written by
Charis Mather

KidHaven
PUBLISHING

Published in 2027 by
KidHaven Publishing, an Imprint of Greenhaven Publishing, LLC
2544 Clinton St., Buffalo, NY 14224

Written by: Charis Mather
Edited by: Beth Latham
Designed by: Rob Delph

Cataloging-in-Publication Data
Names: Mather, Charis, 1999-.
Title: Herbs / Charis Mather.
Description: Buffalo, NY : KidHaven Publishing, 2027. | Series: A kid's guide to growing... | Includes glossary and index.
Identifiers: ISBN 9781534569898 (pbk.) | ISBN 9781534569904 (library bound) | ISBN 9781534569911 (ebook)
Subjects: LCSH: Herbs--Juvenile literature.
Classification: LCC SB351.M38 2027 | DDC 615.321--dc23

Printed in China

CPSIA compliance information: Batch #QS27KH: For further information contact Greenhaven Publishing LLC at 1-844-317-7404.

Please visit our website, www.greenhavenpublishing.com.
For a free color catalog of all our high-quality books, call toll free 1-844-317-7404 or fax 1-844-317-7405.

Find us on

Image Credits

Images courtesy of Shutterstock.com, unless otherwise stated.
Cover and recurring – eliyashevskiy, Torontotokio, ViDI Studio, Spalnic, GSDesign, wallerichmerciei. 2–3 – Kuznetsov Dmitriy, 9dream studio. 4–5 – mavo, Irina WS. 6–7 – YamabikaY, vandycan, D. Kucharski K. Kucharska, pukao, Lipatova Maryna, beats1. 8–9 – Alex Desanshe, gteschner. 10–11 – marseus, Kuznetsov Dmitriy, Natallia Boroda. 12–13 – Valeri Pavljuk, Bogdan Sonjachnyj. 14–15 – cha_cha, Sergey V Kalyakin. 16–17 – 9dream studio, Irina Starikova1811. 18–19 – Amelia Martin, Lukas Gojda. 20–21 – Melinda Nagy, showcake. 22–23 – New Africa, Jokue-photography, galsand.

CONTENTS

Words that look like <u>this</u> can be found in the glossary on page 24.

GROWING HERBS

Have you ever eaten a meal flavored with delicious herbs? Herbs are wonderful plants that often have a fantastic flavor or smell. They also look great in a garden or on the windowsill.

GET YOUR GARDENING GLOVES ON, AND LET'S GET GROWING!

If you want to grow herbs for yourself, it helps to know what these living things need. Let's find out the science behind each step of growing herbs.

PLANTING THE SEEDS

Many herbs can be grown from <u>cuttings</u>, but they can also be grown from seeds. Although seeds are usually small, they contain everything a plant needs to start growing.

BASIL SEEDS

DILL SEEDS

OREGANO SEEDS

CORIANDER SEEDS

For seeds to sprout, they need water, oxygen, and a good place to grow, such as a seed tray. Put seeds in each section. A clear plastic covering can keep the soil from drying out.

Label each section so you know which herb is which.

WATERING THE SEEDS

Keep a close eye on your herb seeds over the next few weeks. Check the soil regularly. When the soil starts to dry out, you will need to add water.

Different herbs may need different amounts of water.

Some seeds are planted on top of the soil instead of under it. They could get washed away if you add too much water at once. Use a spray bottle to gently water these seeds.

STARTING TO GROW

When a seed sprouts, a stem pushes out of the soil and roots grow down into the soil. The roots help the plant stay in place and collect water and nutrients. The stem begins to grow leaves.

Your seedlings may lean to one side as they grow toward the light. You can turn them regularly so they grow a little straighter.

Take off the clear plastic covering once your seeds have sprouted.

REPOTTING THE HERBS

After a few weeks, your seedlings might outgrow their starter tray or pots. You will need to replant them.

Gently remove the herbs from their pots and loosen the soil around the root ball.

When you plant your herbs in their new home, pat fresh soil around them to help them stay in place. Make sure they have plenty of room to spread their roots.

PROTECTING THE PLANT

As your plants continue to grow, keep checking on them. Sometimes, unwanted bugs might eat your herbs. These are called pests. Use a cloth to gently wipe any pests off. Then, let them go.

One way to keep pests away is to plant flowers that pests do not like the smell of or that attract pest-eating insects. Marigolds and lavender are good at keeping pests away from your herbs.

Many herbs also grow flowers that attract helpful insects.

PRUNING THE HERBS

Some herb trimmings can be used to flavor your food.

Pruning is an important part of growing herbs. Pruning involves cutting back certain parts of the plant, such as leaves. With a little bit of regular pruning, your herbs will grow back healthier and fuller.

When pruning, make sure not to trim off too much at once. Your herbs still need most of their leaves. Different herbs need pruning in different places, so check this before you start cutting.

Pruning uses sharp tools, so ask an adult to help you.

GROWING FLOWERS

Without regular pruning, your herbs may start growing flowers. Instead of using their energy to grow back leaves that have been cut off, they put their energy into the flowers. This makes some herbs less tasty.

Coriander, or cilantro, has bitter flowers.

Sometimes, you may want to let your herbs flower. Their flowers attract insects that pollinate them, which is how they grow seeds. Pollinators are an important part of a healthy garden.

THIS BEE IS POLLINATING A SAGE FLOWER.

SEPARATING THE HERBS

If your herbs are growing too close together, you might want to separate them. When plants grow right next to each other, their roots tend to tangle and clump together.

You can split herbs up to give them more room. Dig around the plant's root ball. Gently pull on the roots to separate the root ball into smaller clumps. Plant the clumps farther apart.

WHAT WILL YOU GROW?

There are all kinds of wonderful herbs you could try growing. You could grow <u>culinary</u> herbs to add to your food. You could grow <u>medicinal</u> herbs, which have lots of different uses.

What kinds of herbs would you like to grow?

Now that you know the steps for growing and caring for herbs, you are ready to start gardening. You can also learn how to dry out your herbs so you can enjoy them for longer!

GLOSSARY

ATTRACT to gain someone or something's interest

CULINARY to do with cooking

CUTTINGS pieces of fully grown plants that can be used to grow new plants

ENERGY the power that makes living things able to move and live

MEDICINAL to do with health and healing

NUTRIENTS natural substances that plants and animals need to take in to grow and stay healthy

OXYGEN a natural gas that living things need in order to survive

POLLINATE to pass on pollen from a plant to another plant of the same kind so that seeds will be produced

REGULARLY consistently

ROOT BALL a bunch of roots grown by a plant

INDEX